My Amazing Toddler
Behavioral Series

# I Say "Nighty, Night".

# I GO TO BED!

### An Affirmation-Themed Toddler Book
### About Going to Bed (Ages 2-4)

By

Suzanne T. Christian

TWORAVENS
B O O K S

**Two Little Ravens**
CHILDREN'S NON-FICTION BOOKS

Paperback Edition: 9781964202655
Hardcover Edition: 9781964202662
Digital Edition: 9781964202679

Published in the United States by Two Ravens Books LLC,
254 Chapman Rd, Ste 209, Newark DE 19702

'Expand the mind, free the imagination, one title at a time.'
www.tworavensbooks.com

# Welcome to

# "I Say "Nighty, Night."
# I Go To Bed!"

## A Calming, Affirmation-Themed Bedtime Book for Toddlers.

This gentle resource is crafted to help toddlers feel safe, confident, and ready for sleep. With simple affirmations and playful bedtime routines, each page creates a sense of comfort and familiarity that little ones can rely on night after night.

Intended for 2 to 4-year-olds, the book pairs snug illustrations with calming text to help them learn emotional control and achieve bedtime independence. Reading after a warm bath or cuddling with a teddy, these calming words make bedtime the best part of your child's day.

Reading this book together regularly will create sweet nighttime memories and lay the foundation for lifelong emotional wellness.

Sweet dreams start here.

Suzanne T. Christian

My bath is done;
I smell like bubbles.

I brush my teeth.
shine, shine, shine, shine!

Pajamas on,
**zip, zip!**
I go to bed!

I pick up a book;
stories in bed make me sleepy.

Teddy hugs me tight;
we're brave together.

Lights get low;
the room feels cozy.

I take a deep breath, in and out.
I'm ready for dreamland.

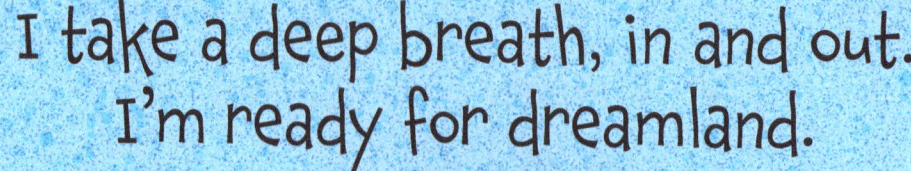

I am safe. I am calm.
I'm ready for bed.

I wave to the moon
**night-night,
moon!**

My night-light glows
like a tiny star.

I tell my toys, "Sleep tight, friends."

I count three sheep
**boing, boing, boing**
then sleep.

Pillow soft as clouds under my head. I go to bed!

I float on a dream cloud
**whee!**

I am brave! I'm not afraid of the dark; monsters are not real.

I wiggle my toes, I close my eyes. I go to bed!

I am brave,
I am calm,
I am loved.

I Say
"Nighty, Night".

I Go To
BED!

The End!

# My Amazing Toddler Behavioral Series

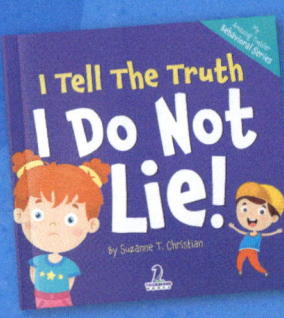

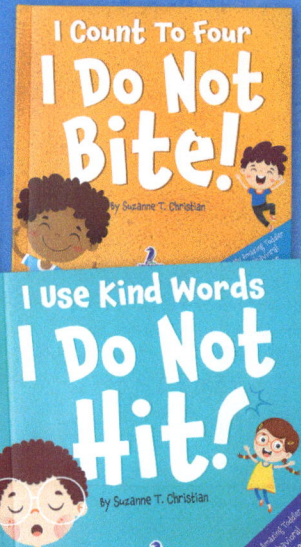

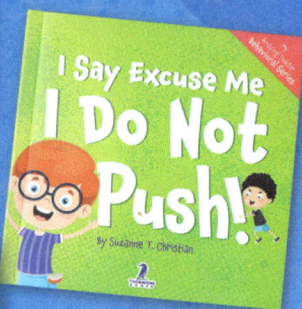

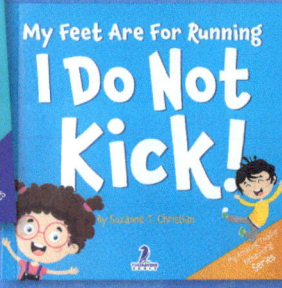

Check Out
Suzanne T. Christian's beloved series
'My Amazing Toddler Behavioral Series'.
Young readers are sure to enjoy!

Two Little Ravens
CHILDREN'S NON-FICTION BOOKS

## Dear Amazing Reader,

Thank you for diving into **I Say "Nighty, Night." I Go to Bed!**. with me. If this book touched your heart or made a difference for a young reader, I'd be grateful if you could share your thoughts in a review. Your feedback inspires my future work and helps others discover the magic within these pages.

I'd love to hear from you directly if you have suggestions or ideas for improving the book. Please feel free to reach out to me at **suzanne.christian@tworavensbooks.com.** Your voice counts, and I cherish it deeply.

With heartfelt gratitude,